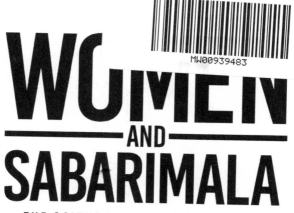

WOMEN
AND
SABARIMALA
THE SCIENCE BEHIND RESTRICTIONS

SINU JOSEPH

INDIA • SINGAPORE • MALAYSIA

Notion Press

Old No. 38, New No. 6
McNichols Road, Chetpet
Chennai - 600 031

First Published by Notion Press 2019
Copyright © Sinu Joseph 2019
All Rights Reserved.

ISBN 978-1-64733-633-2

Dedication

Smt. Vyjayanthi Krishnamurthy
(June 25, 1962 – Oct 03, 2019)

*This book is dedicated to the loving memory of
Smt. Vyjayanthi Krishnamurthy, without whose presence
this journey would not have materialized.*

CONTENTS

————— ✕⊰⊱✕ —————

FOREWORD

I feel privileged in writing a foreword to the book "Women and Sabarimala - The Science Behind Restrictions" by Sinu Joseph.

The Vedas declare the nature of the Supreme Truth in many ways. According to me, the supreme truth is Lord Sastha himself: *"Sastha adhipathir vo asthu"* (Sastha is the ultimate ruler), says Yajur Veda.

Only blessed souls can think, contemplate and have devotion towards this Supreme power. The worship of Sastha was found throughout the world in ancient times, but after the subjugation of Hinduism in the North after Islamic invasion and rule, both worship of Sastha and his philosophy were restricted to the south.

My Lord Bhakta Paripala gave me the duty of writing "Shri Maha Sastha Vijayam". I completed the work after a detailed research of 14 years. Worship of Sastha is not confined to Sabarimala alone. Lord Sastha, as a Yogeeswara, His dynamic power awakens spiritual cognition to propel souls onward in their evolution to their origin.

antarmukha samArAdyA – says Lalitha Sahasranama. Inner accomplishment is the real sadhana. But for normal humans, it is not an easy task and hence specific temples evolved for this purpose.

The six temples which are dear to Lord Sastha signify the six *chakra*s in the human body through which the *Kundalini* rises to travel to the Supreme State. This inner journey of *Kundalini* is indicated with an outer journey of temples. It is an inner fulfillment, arrived at after an outer journey.

"yata: piNDANDe tata: brahmANDe

yata: brahmANDe tata piNDANDe"

That which is there inside the body, is there in the cosmos.

That which is there in the cosmos, is there inside the body.

There is a perfect equation between human existence and the external world. Based on this idea, I wrote an article a few years ago, on "The Six Sastha Temples and the Shat Chakras".

Sinu Joseph, the author, once called me over phone and spoke to me regarding this article. Sinu, Managing

Trustee of Myrthi Speaks Trust, is doing a yeomen service by working on issues including menstrual health and sanitation. Though I have been working with the Sabarimala case with several organizations, when Sinu called me, I was really surprised in what way I'm connected to the area with which she is already doing a commendable job.

When we met, I was very much intrigued when she told me that after reading the article, she had ventured into visiting all these temples in person. She took all the pains and came down to Coimbatore to meet me to get better clarity on my article. Her quest for truth has resulted in this book.

I have been visiting these temples right from my childhood. Though being a writer or speaker, I'm also a *sadhaka* and the way I approach these places, apart from textual references, is based on my personal experience. But it is really amazing to see the entire scenario from a woman's perspective. Though *Kundalini* is about spiritual journey of *Jeevatma*, the physical body in a specific cycle of life is definitely in two different planes for a male and female. The author has tried to explore that, experience that, and record the same.

For instance, her experience at Aryankavu (which she has recorded in this book) still fascinates me. She compares the energy there as to how it impacts men and women. She talks about the force there - "that gives a significant pull for men". My tryst with Aryankavu started with an experience akin to this at the age of five. The way the author has penned it down about how the grove of grace transforms the universal, human plane and earthly forces into life-force energy - definitely deserves appreciation beyond doubt.

There is no doubt that this book will be a valuable document. It will not only be benefiting the devotees but also the public who wish to understand the reality behind the concept of Ayyappa.

I wish the worth-while venture all success.

With my prayers to His holy feet.

– V. Aravind Subramanyam

President, Shri Maha Sasthru Seva Sangam

Coimbatore

PREFACE

———— ✕❖✕ ————

Sabarimala and Me

I have been a menstrual health educator in rural India for a decade. One might wonder what business I have writing about Sabarimala because my area of work seems poles apart from a temple like Sabarimala, which is meant largely for male devotees. In fact, for those unaware, Sabarimala's restriction on entry of women in the menstruating age, is the case which piqued my interest and made me venture into this adventure. I call it an adventure, because it revealed certain aspects of faith and science that I stumbled upon, unknowingly.

What brought the case of Sabarimala into my purview was how it was pushed into limelight by menstrual activists. Movements such as "Happy to Bleed" by menstrual advocates demanded that the legal system of India remove the restriction on entry of women in the menstrual age. What they might not have thought is that if women in the menstruating age entered Sabarimala, there is very little chance that they will continue to feel happy to bleed. Why?

This book explores the possible answers to that Why.

Science and Religion

One of the biggest learning for me has been the existence of a deep connection that I repeatedly encountered, between indigenous science and religion. Every time I dug deeper to get to the root of menstrual restrictions with respect to religion, it invariably took me to India's native knowledge systems – *Ayurveda, Tantra, Chakras* and *Agama Shastra*, to name a few. Without the knowledge of the fundamental principles guiding these systems, their interconnection and especially their impact on the human physiology, it is not possible to comprehend such restrictions. The lack of understanding the science behind these knowledge systems is the reason why we find such difficulty in understanding our cultural and religious practices.

India's native sciences understand life at a subtle level. In the language known to modern science, one might term this as meta-science or the quantum understanding of existence. However, in India itself, there have been large periods of discontinuity in constant exploration and research on these subjects, owing to the systematic destruction of native knowledge systems during the colonial and pre-colonial times.

In recent times, while branches of physics, chemistry and even mathematics have expanded on the understanding as well as application of science at the quantum level, life sciences and modern medicine are years away from taking to the subject of Quantum Biology. Modern medicine seems very content with the outdated atom and molecule theory and seems in no rush to understand human physiology at the sub-atomic level. Although there are niche application areas such as DNA mutation, day-to-day diagnosis and treatment of disease is far from applying quantum understanding of life.

What would it be like if modern medicine uses quantum biology for diagnosis of disease? Well, it would be very much like Ayurveda and the Chakra system. This is the science upon which the Hindu religion, culture and temples are based. Therefore, it will be through the lens of India's native sciences that the restriction on women, in the reproductive age, in Sabarimala, will be explored in this book. It goes without saying that even to dismiss what is written here, one needs to have a fundamental understanding of such sciences, because the lens of modern medicine will invariably fall short at this point in time.

Religion and Experience

How do we know that something is true?

Most people know it through second hand information – data, numbers and expert opinions. There is another way to know things - firsthand information gained through direct experience. This is one of the ways in which one can genuinely separate fact from fiction. More importantly, it is direct experience that can shape religious understanding. My understanding is based on this. In this book, I have shared my personal experiences of visiting five temples associated with Sabarimala and how it impacted me as a woman. I have not visited the Sabarimala shrine, although the Supreme Court of India has removed the restrictions on women (as of 2018), not only out of respect for the wishes of devotees, but also because my experiences with other temples has made me understand what such a space can do to women in the menstruating age. I have attempted to describe my experiences through the language of India's native sciences.

What does it take to experience the nature of that, which permeates a temple?

They say that some people are born with the ability to experience the subtle realm. In India, we call this *Purva Janma Samskara*. However, I am not one of them. For most people like me, it is of utmost necessity to train the body and mind to be able to experience subtle phenomena. Regular practice of yoga, pranayama and meditation will go a long way in preparing ourselves to experience subtle aspects of life.

Our body is the tool with which we can have profound experiences, provided it is not ridden with disease. For example, a woman whose menstrual cycle is already disturbed and painful, will not be able to distinguish the impact of breaking cultural restrictions pertaining to menstruation. Similarly, a mind that is constantly turned outward towards material pursuits, is restless and always insecure, will not be able to tune itself to the subtler aspects. If we wish to have firsthand experiences of the subtle realm, we need to quieten the inner chatter. All the answers that we seek are within us. They only emerge when we practice utter silence.

That is why, in the Hindu culture, religion is always associated with austerities to discipline the body and quieten the mind, thereby helping us turn inward. We see this in great detail in the Sabarimala tradition.

The purpose of sharing my experiences in such detail is because I would like others to know that it is possible for them too, to walk into a temple and experience it. It is only through such experiences that we can have a glimpse of how some spaces like Sabarimala can negatively impact women's health.

Understanding Sabarimala holistically

I fully resonate with the phrase of Newton that "one can only see further than others by standing on the shoulders of giants". In this case, the enormous research and writings of Shri V. Aravind Subramanyam on Sastha and Sabarimala has been the guiding light for my work. His expertise comes not only from research, but also from his direct experience, and that is what sets his knowledge apart. His writing on the *Shat-Chakra* temples associated with Sabarimala is what set me on this journey to understand the Sabarimala tradition holistically. I thank him from the bottom of my heart for pointing me in the direction in which to seek answers.

In areas where I fall short of understanding, I claim full responsibility. In areas where you may resonate with what I have written, I give credit to the Grace that made it possible for me to see beyond the obvious and find words to express it. No matter how much one claims to have knowledge, it has been my experience that without Her Grace, nothing is possible.

———

ACKNOWLEDGEMENTS

This book would not have been possible without the research and in-dept understanding of Lord Sastha and Ayyappa, expounded in the many works of Shri V. Aravind Subramanyam. I am immensely grateful to him for his willingness to guide me, proof-read this work, provide images of Lord Sastha for this book and also for writing the Foreword, despite his very busy schedule.

To my co-partners in this journey, Bhaskar and Vyjayanthi, I extend much gratitude for their unending support and encouragement to get such a work out. I thank Bhaskar also for taking the time out to proof-read the manuscript and offer valuable suggestions, without which the book would not have been the same.

Finally, to all the women who raised the question - "Why are we not allowed to enter Sabarimala?" – your questions have taken me on this journey. For that, I thank you.

CHAPTER 1

THE SCIENCE OF HINDU TEMPLES

"What is here is elsewhere. What is not here, is nowhere"

– Vishvasāra Tantra

(Yad ihāsti tad anyatra, yannehāsti na tat kvachit)

Spirituality is not the same as religion. Religion involving the worship of *Devis* and *Devatas*, or feminine and masculine deities, are various forms of energies which are a means to an end; the end being, spiritual liberation or enlightenment. Just as every destination has several routes, so also, the spiritual path has various means of reaching the end. Religion and devotion that we associate with temples, is one of the methods. Yoga, in its many forms, is another.

In Hindu tradition, we understand the evolution of human existence as part of the four *Yugas* or epoch ages, namely the *Krta Yuga, Treta Yuga, Dvapara Yuga* and *Kali Yuga*. With each *Yuga*, the human capacity for self-realization is said to decline. The current *Kali Yuga* is considered as the most degenerate, with humans having degraded in morality and virtue. In the 12-volume book, The Agama Encyclopedia, by S.K Ramachandra Rao[1], he writes: "In the *puranas*, it is said that

* In *Krta Yuga*, there were no temples as God appeared and helped people directly.

* In *Treta Yuga*, virtue diminished, and God appeared in their own normal forms (for the virtuous folk) as well as in iconic forms (for others). But still there were no temples, as people installed icons in their homes for worship (*grha-pratistha*).

* In *Dwapara-yuga*, when virtue and vice almost vied with each other, sages installed idols in remote forests, for those who were willing to take the trouble to visit such places.

* In *Kali Yuga*, when vice is more than virtue, there is a need for a temple in every town and village, as it is only the divine presence in icon form that can help during this degenerate period."

Temples are said to date back to a time of third or fourth century after Christ. This explains why Ayurveda texts which are dated much earlier, have no mention of menstrual restrictions for temple visits.

---

1 The Agama Encyclopedia, by S.K. Ramachandra Rao

Tantra

Hindu temples, as we know them today, are designed specifically for the *Kali Yuga*, keeping in mind that in this *Yuga*, it is difficult for human beings to pursue the paths of pure Yoga for self-realization. And thus, the science of Tantra came into being.

The Vedas propounded the highest truth (*Jnana Kanda*) and means for self-realization through *yajna*[2], strict discipline and austerity (*Karma Kanda*). The attaining of *mukthi* (liberation) was to be the goal of every individual. However, in the *Kali Yuga*, people's priorities changed and *bhukti* (enjoyment) became more important than *mukthi*. People became so caught up in worldly affairs, that it became impossible to discuss or teach higher spiritual realities that lead to *mukthi*. Therefore, Tantra came into being which ensured that people could obtain *bhukthi* and yet, attain *mukthi*. Hindu temples are exemplary evidences of this principle.

Tantra, in its simplest definition, means technique. All Hindu temples are designed with the knowledge of Tantra. The *Agama Shastras* which provide details for temple construction, consecration, worship and ritual procedures are rooted in the science of Tantra. Tantra is a deep and vast science; yet it is very experiential. All those who visit a Hindu temple will have a firsthand

---

2 Yajna refers to ancient rituals performed with a specific objective

experience of how the science of Tantra can impact the human body and mind.

Temples and the Human Body

When we pursue spiritual enlightenment through pure Yoga based on Vedanta, we turn inwards with full awareness. Yoga is not just about the twisting and turning of the body into various postures, as is propagated in recent times. Yoga is about complete union with the cosmic energies, and one of the methods is *Hatha Yoga*, which is the popular method comprising *asanas* (postures). The other methods include *Jnana Yoga*, the path of pursuing ultimate truth through knowledge; *Raja Yoga*, the pursuit of truth by gaining control over the mind; *Bhakti Yoga*, which is pure devotion; *Karma Yoga*, which is the art of being detached while pursuing a life of action; *Laya Yoga* (also called *Kundalini Yoga*), which provides techniques of pranayama and meditation to energize the *chakras* and raise the *kundalini*; and *Mantra Yoga*, which refers to the use of *mantras* to attain liberation. No one method is superior to the other. All are equally potent and valid methods to reach the ultimate goal.

Yoga draws upon the individual's capacity to overcome physical and mental limitations and go beyond the body and mind. In this path, also called the *nivritti marg*, temple visits and *Devi-Devata* worship becomes secondary (or non-existent), and the focus is on the individual's ability to cross human barriers, break the birth and rebirth cycles, and attain *mukthi*. The idea of God in such a path is *Nirguna*, that is, without attributes, and as being pure Divine Consciousness. This is a very difficult path, as what one pursues is formless, and hence difficult to grasp within the limitations of the five senses. Naturally, only a small percentage of people take to such a path. The alternative available for all humans is that of Hindu temples and the *Saguna* aspect of God, in which the deity manifests in a form that human beings can relate to. Worship of deities refers to the *Saguna* aspect.

Regardless of whether the path chosen is *Nirguna* or *Saguna*, every spiritual process has a corresponding physiological impact. By replicating the human physiology in a Hindu temple, it becomes possible for the temple to expand the human consciousness, just as Yoga would. Our body is a replica of the macrocosm, and whatever is contained in the macrocosm, is also contained within the human body. This is what is meant by the quote in Vishvasaara Tantra,

"What is here is there. What is not here, is nowhere."

Hindu temples help us connect to the larger cosmos in this manner. That too, with minimal effort on our part, with the only requirement that we visit the temple as per the rules laid down. Yes, that is how simple the entire process has been made for humans in the *Kali Yuga*. All that is required of humans is for them to walk in to the consecrated spaces, and allow it to have an impact on them.

The *Agama Shastras* teach how the temple is to be built similar to the human body. In fact, the *Vastu Mandala*, which is the diagram providing the basis for architectural design of the temple, is depicted with a human-like person lying facing the ground. This person is called the *Vastu Purusha*, the Cosmic Man. Through the body of the *Vastu Purusha*, we learn how the body of the temple too comprises similar sections as that of a human being.[3]

S.K. Ramachandra Rao's book[4] explains how the ancient texts compare the temple to the likeness of a human form: "As a temple is laid out, it is said to picture a man (the *Vastu Purusha*) lying down. His feet connote the entrance tower, his genital organ the flag-staff (*dhvaja-stambha*), his belly the assembly hall (*ranga mandapa*), his heart the porch (*antarala*), his head the sanctum and the brow-meet (space between eyebrows) the seat of the icon."

How exactly do temples replicate the human physiology? Is it just symbolic, or is it more? And how does it impact us at the physical level?

In order to answer these questions, it is time we explore the fascinating subtle science of *Chakras*, as expounded in the Tantra texts.

---

3 The Hindu Temple Vol 1, 1946, by Stella Kramrisch
4 The Agama Encyclopedia: Alaya and Aradhana, by S.K. Ramachandra Rao

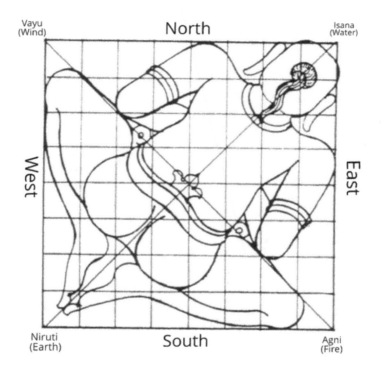

Figure 1: Vastu Purusha Mandala

(Image Source: By Verena Rapp de Eston - Own work, CC BY-SA 4.0,
httpscommons.wikimedia.orgwindex.phpcurid=43730422)

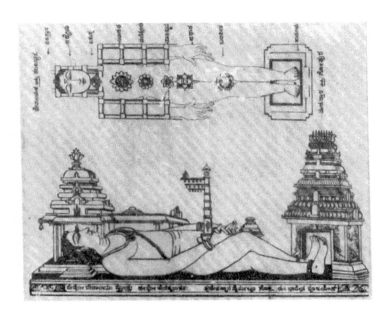

Figure 2: Manushya Devalaya,
(Source: Rao, S.K.Ramachandra. The Agama Encyclopedia, 2005)

Chakras

The techniques employed in creating a consecrated space have an impact on the human body through the subtle energy junctions called *chakras*. In order to understand how Tantra works with respect to temples, it is a must to understand how *chakras* influence the human body.

Chakras and their effect on us, depend on our preparedness and desire of pursuing a particular path. If we pursue the *pravritti marg* (path of action), then the influence of *chakras* will be at the physical level, to ensure worldly comforts, good health and wellbeing. If we pursue the *nivritti* marg (path of renunciation), then *chakras* will influence us at a spiritual level, turning our journey inwards and towards liberation. That is why, in many instances, we see the same temples offering worldly comforts for some, and spiritual possibilities for another.

Since it is easier to start with what we already know, let us first look at how *chakras* correspond to the human anatomy, as per modern medicine. I will also touch upon how *chakras* impact *doshas* as per Ayurveda. The subsequent chapters will throw light on how the same *chakras* correspond to the spiritual aspects.

Chakras and Human Anatomy

Human anatomy as understood through modern medicine, has a corresponding subtle anatomy that is understood in the *chakra* system and Ayurveda.

At the physical level, most of us are familiar with what nerves and plexus points are. Plexus are junctions where nerve fibers meet, exchange and then branch out to specific parts of the body. The spinal plexus includes the cervical plexus, the brachial plexus, the lumbar plexus, the sacral plexus and the coccygeal plexus, encompassing regions from the top of the spine to the base of the spine. Apart from this, we have autonomic plexus which include the cardiac plexus, the pulmonary plexus, the solar plexus, and so on.

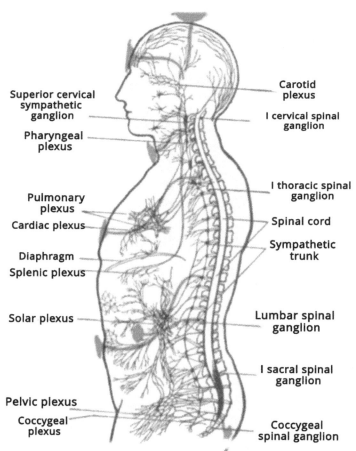

Superior cervical sympathetic ganglion

Pharyngeal plexus

Pulmonary plexus

Cardiac plexus

Diaphragm

Splenic plexus

Solar plexus

Pelvic plexus

Coccygeal plexus

Carotid plexus

I cervical spinal ganglion

I thoracic spinal ganglion

Spinal cord

Sympathetic trunk

Lumbar spinal ganglion

I sacral spinal ganglion

Coccygeal spinal ganglion

Chakras and the nervous system

Figure 3: Nerve Plexus and Chakras

(Source: Leadbeater, C.W. Chakras, 1927)

Note that the author mentions a Spleen Chakra and omits Swadisthana Chakra in his book and in this image.)

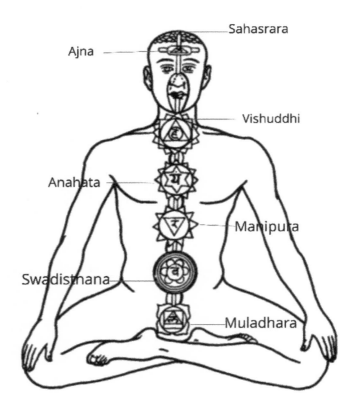

Figure 4: Location of Chakras
(Source: Swami Sivananda. Kundalini Yoga. 1994)

Just as there are nerves and plexus which function at the gross level, there are *nadis* and *chakras*, which function at the subtle level. Ayurveda texts indicate the presence of around 72,000 *nadis* which act as subtle energy channels. The points or junctions where several *nadis* meet is called a *chakra*. Five of the *chakras* (from *Muladhara* to *Vishuddhi*) operate in the *Pranamaya Kosha* (energy sheath), while the sixth, *Ajna Chakra,* and intermediary *chakras* up to the *Sahasrara*, operate at the *Manomaya Kosha* (mental sheath). The seventh, *Sahasrara* is not actually a *chakra*, but rather the state of pure Consciousness.

Although invisible to the outer eye, *chakras* do not operate in isolation, and its sphere of influence encompasses specific plexus, endocrine glands[5] and organs that correspond to it. Although *chakras* are operational in all human beings, it is more active and capable of channelizing greater energy in one who is spiritually evolved or proactively works on energizing the *chakras*.

Doshas[6] that operate in specific regions of the body are also influenced by the corresponding *chakras*

---

5 Endocrine glands help hormones communicate with each other, thereby regulating and controlling various functions within the body.

6 Doshas – Ayurveda recognizes three primary doshas (subtle biological forces) that influence all functioning within the body. They are Vata Dosha, Pitta Dosha and Kapha Dosha.

in that region. Ayurveda texts describe three primary biological forces or *doshas* called *Vata, Pitta* and *Kapha.* In this context, it is necessary to understand the sub-types of *Vata dosha* in some detail, since it has an important role in menstruation and reproductive activity.

Vata dosha regulates and maintains all movements in the body, including the movements of inhalation and exhalation, the movement of food in the digestive tract, the excretion of wastes, the flow of menstrual blood and also the process of birthing. The five sub-types of Vata dosha are Prana, Udana, Vyana, Samana and Apana. Their directions and regions of operation within the body are shown in figure 5. Each of these also correspond to a particular chakra and are influenced by it. In turn, the *doshas* influence the various functions that they manage.

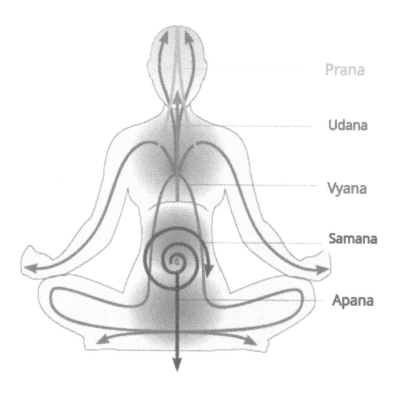

Prana

Udana

Vyana

Samana

Apana

Figure 5: Sub-types of Vata Dosha
(original source unknown)

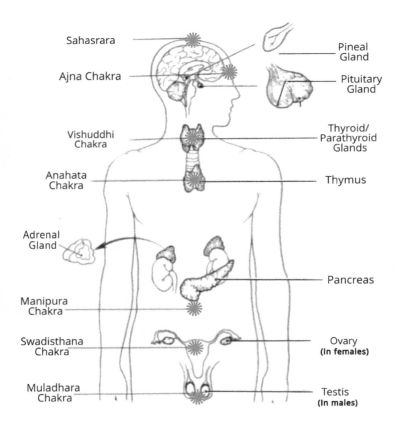

Figure 6: Chakras and Endocrine Glands

2. Swadisthana chakra

Swa means Self, and *adhisthana* means seat. *Swadisthana* refers to the seat of the Supreme Self. It is where *Shakti*, the primordial feminine force, resides. This is the second *chakra* from the base of the spine.

Location: Root of the genitals

Plexus: *Swadisthana chakra* correspond to the sacral plexus that arise from the lower back just above the sacrum. The sacral plexus provides motor and sensory nerves for the pelvis, thigh, knee, calf and foot.

Gland: Ovaries in females and testes in males

Dosha: *Apana Vayu*

Element: *Varuna* (water)

Influence: Functions of the *Swadisthana chakra* are closely associated with functions of the *muladhara chakra*. While *muladhara* is largely associated with the basic survival, *swadishthana* is mainly associated with procreative abilities. When it is not sufficiently energized, it impacts the functioning of ovaries in women, thereby causing menstrual and reproductive health disorders. The *muladhara* and *swadishthana chakras* are essential for proper functioning of the downward moving *Apana Vayu* which directs the flow of menstrual blood and aids the process of birthing. Any change in direction of *Apana Vayu* or blockages in its movement could result in menstrual and reproductive disorders for women.

Temples: *Devi* temples associated with fertility, are examples of temples that work to energize the *Swadisthana chakra* and rectify any alterations in the *apana vayu*, thereby resolving problems of infertility and other reproductive health issues. Such temples are often associated with ensuring good health, fertility and well-being.

3. Manipura chakra

Mani refers to a precious gem, and *pura* is the term used to denote a region or town. Therefore, *manipura* refers to the land of the precious gem, indicating wealth and prosperity. This is the third *chakra* from the base of the spine.

Location: It is situated in the root/base of the navel

Plexus: *Manipura chakra* corresponds to the region of the Solar plexus

Gland: Adrenal Glands and Pancreas

Dosha: *Samana Vayu*

Element: *Agni* (fire)

Influence: *Manipura chakra* regulates the functions of digestion and assimilation of food. Energizing the *manipura chakra* increases the digestive fire, *pitta*, which not only aids physical digestion of food, but also provides the fire power to pursue worldly goals. This *chakra* also regulates the *samana vayu*, which is responsible for digestion and assimilation of food. Those who are active in this *chakra* would often have an aggressive personality and an ambitious nature. This *chakra* provides the ambition and drive to do well in worldly affairs.

Temples: Temples which work to energize the *manipura chakra* equip devotees in the *pravritti marg* with the fire (*agni*) required to fulfill worldly desires and achieve materialistic goals. The element of *Agni* is powerful in these temples. For those on the spiritual path, *manipura chakra* is the start of the process of renunciation. The Umananda temple in Guwahati (Assam) is an example where one can experience the spiritual aspects of this *chakra*.

4. Anahata chakra

Anahata refers to unstruck sound. That is, sound which is not produced by clanging of two objects.

Location: It is situated in the region of the heart.

Plexus: *Anahata chakra* corresponds to the cardiac plexus.

Gland: Thymus gland

Dosha: *Vyana Vayu*

Element: *Vayu* (air)

Influence: Energizing the *anahata chakra* takes the person towards a more compassionate and inclusive way of living, rather than being only materialistic. It also helps in dispelling fear. When this *chakra* is active, being kind and exuding compassion becomes effortless. *Anahata chakra* influences the *Vyana Vayu* which is responsible for maintaining circulation and balancing the other *vayus* in the body.

Temples: Temples that energize the *anahata chakra* are powerful centres of overcoming fear and having desires fulfilled. Several *Bhadrakali* and *Durga* temples trigger the *anahata chakra*, removing the cause of fear and granting devotees their wishes.

5. Vishuddhi chakra

Vishudhhi means highly pure or a purifying filter.

Location: It is situated in the region of the neck, at the base of the throat.

Plexus: It corresponds to the cervical plexus which governs the regions of neck, head and shoulders. It also corresponds to the region of the pharynx and larynx, and therefore, the pharyngeal and laryngeal plexus.

Gland: Thyroid and Parathyroid gland

Dosha: *Udana Vayu*

Element: *Akasha* (space/ether)

Influence: At the physical level, activation of the *vishuddhi chakra* helps with problems pertaining to the thyroid gland and the throat region. Improved speech, articulation and creativity are associated with this *chakra*. *Vishuddhi chakra* also influences the role of the *Udana Vayu* which is responsible for exhalation and speech.

consecration. The *prana prathistha*, that is, the process of consecrating an idol is how the priest infuses life and *chaitanyam* into the idol, making it a *vigraham*. The term *chaitanyam* or *chaitanya* is often used in South Indian languages, to describe the nature of that which is consecrated in a temple. The type of *chaitanyam* in a temple determines the effect it has on humans.

The architecture of the temples further ensures that this *chaitanyam* could be stored and directed towards devotees. The interesting part is that every temple could have a different *chaitanyam*, even if the worshipped deity is the same, as we see with the *shat-chakra* temples associated with Sabarimala. Only the chief priest who was involved in consecrating the temple would fully know what exactly he put in there. The *Sankalpa*, or the intention that is put into each *vigraham* is what decides the rituals to be performed for each temple. Simplified versions of explanations is passed on to devotees through stories associated with the temple, so that the rituals performed would upkeep the intended *chaitanyam*.

Physiology of Liberation

All spiritual practices aim at raising the coiled *kundalini* energy from the *muladhara chakra* at the base of the spine, towards the *sahasrara chakra* which is located above the brain, near the pineal gland. This is the physiological impact of working towards liberation.

The *kundalini* is considered as a type of coiled energy (and hence the association with a coiled serpent) that lies dormant in the *muladhara chakra*. Once it is aroused, it will rise and pierce through each *chakra* on its way up. As the *kundalini* passes through each *chakra*, the practitioner will experience the manifestation of various qualities associated with that *chakra*, both physically and spiritually.

Thus, we see that Hindu temples based on *Agama Shastra* are closely related to *chakras* and their subtle influence on the human body and mind, fulfilling worldly desires and yet, guiding one towards the ultimate liberation. With this fundamental knowledge, we can now begin exploring the *shat-chakra* temples associated with Sabarimala.

CHAPTER 2

WOMEN AND SABARIMALA

※⟶⟨≫⟩⟵※

As a child, I remember visiting my native place in Palakkad, Kerala, every summer. There were two things I learnt from those visits. One was *"Inqalab Zindabad"*[8] the slogan of red flag protestors, we often saw marching past our homes. And the other was *"Swamiye Saranam Ayyappa!"*, the slogan of Ayyappa devotees. When nobody watched, I used to imitate the slogan shouters, in my own childish way, tying a red scarf on my head and marching around the house. With equal fervor, I recall carrying some towels on my head (to resemble the *Irrumudi*) and going in circles shouting *Swamiye Ayyappo! Ayyappo Swamiye!* As a child, I never understood what *Inqalab Zindabad* could mean. It also never occurred to me that I am a Catholic and Ayyappa is a Hindu deity. It was simply an aspect of being from Kerala. I never could have imagined that

---

8 Inqalab Zindabad is the translated version of 'Long Live the Russian Revolution'. This was a slogan of the Communist Party in Kerala.

the intermingling of these two slogans would create such unrest in Kerala.

Swamiye Saranam Ayyappa is a slogan that still leaves me with goosebumps. That overwhelming quality of Sabarimala's Lord Ayyappa is what draws crores of men every year to this pilgrim site. It is only natural, that at some point, the question would be raised as to why women were not allowed to be a part of this experience. More specifically, why women in the reproductive age (10 to 50 years), were restricted from entering Sabarimala.

My efforts to understand the reason behind these restrictions began in early 2016, when there was much noise about a certain group that went to court asking the law to intervene and remove the restrictions on women's entry in Sabarimala, citing reasons of inequality. In 2018, the Supreme Court enforced removal of the restriction and said that women in the menstruating age (10 to 50 years) can no longer be restricted from entering Sabarimala. The ruling Communist party (CPI-M) in Kerala went a step ahead and attempted to proactively bring in women, much against the wishes of the traditional devotees. This led to a series of protests by devotees, including women devotees, who felt that it was a violation of the right to practice religion and follow tradition as per one's desire. Most of the voices for and against this have been politically driven, leaving the common women with more questions than answers. Why haven't we been able to give women the straightforward reason as to why they are restricted from entering Sabarimala?

As part of my study on this subject, I had interviewed Smt. Devika Devi at her home in Chengannur, sometime in 2016. She is the mother of the then *Thantri* (chief priest) in Sabarimala. She is a gentle, soft spoken woman, who told me in a quiet voice that women do not realize how visiting Sabarimala is not good for their health. Unfortunately, her voice was never heard in the mainstream media, as the representatives of this case were largely men who made it about a celibate deity not wanting women around him. As a woman, I am not surprised that many women would find such remarks insulting. As someone who deeply respects Lord Ayyappa and the traditions in Sabarimala, I find it even more painful that such discrimination is ascribed to Him.

The *Shat Chakras* associated with Sabarimala

We can know a variety of things through theory, history and mythology. But it pales in comparison to what we can discover through experience. Although I had theorized the nature of Sabarimala based on the rituals and written about it in my blog[9], I was not sure

---

9   www.mythrispeaks.wordpress.com 'Sabarimala Story: Can visiting temples affect menstruating women?', 2016 and 'Sabarimala Verdict: Fabricated rights over real experiences of women', 2018

how to confirm if what I was thinking was indeed right. When I decided to write about Sabarimala in this book, I wondered if I could do justice in writing about a place that I had never visited. But at the same time, I was not willing to break tradition and force an entry to the temple, even if the court said otherwise.

I was able to break this catch-22 situation when I chanced upon the work of Shri V. Aravind Subramanyam and his blog titled "The Six Sastha Temples and the Shat Chakras[10]". He has done extensive research on Lord Sastha and Sabarimala. His book *Shri Maha Sastha Vijayam* (currently in Tamil), is an important read for anyone interested in deep research on the Sastha tradition. For me, his blog presented a way to understand Lord Ayyappa through the experience of the five Sastha temples associated with Sabarimala. According to Aravind*ji*, all Ayyappa devotees are ideally required to visit the five temples in a specific order, before going to Sabarimala which is the sixth temple. He says that each of these six temples are said to trigger a specific *chakra* from the *muladhara* to the *ajna*, with Sabarimala being associated with the *ajna chakra*. All my theoretical knowledge about *chakra*s and temples was going to be put to test, because here were six temples associated with the six *chakra*s!

10 www.shanmatha.blogspot.com The Six Sastha Temples and the Shat Chakras

For these visits, I was fortunate to have the company of Bhaskar and Vyjayanthi, my co-partners in most studies of this nature. We visited the first four temples in June 2019. A few months later in September of the same year, Bhaskar and I visited the fifth temple. These experiences helped us concretize everything we had known about the science of temples and understand Sabarimala in a whole new light.

In the following chapters, with each temple, the role of *chakras*, as described in the *Shat-Chakra-Nirupana* text by Swami Purnananda, will also be presented. Swami Purnananda was a celebrated Tantra scholar from Bengal who wrote this text somewhere around 1526 CE. According to this ancient text, each *chakra* is represented as a lotus with a specific colour, shape, element, specific number of petals, specific alphabet/letter for each petal and a seed mantra. There is also a specific male and female deity attributed to each *chakra*. It is interesting to observe that the qualities triggered for one in the *pravritti marg* is often similar to that of the female deity in the *chakras*, while the aspects that open up for one in the *nivritti marg* is similar to that of the male deity in that *chakra*. We shall briefly touch upon both. For details of each *chakra* and its symbolism, it is best to refer the *Shat Chakra Nirupana* text.

However, it is strictly not recommended to attempt energizing the *chakras* without the guidance of a *Guru* as it could badly misfire if not done correctly. This is also the reason why Ayyappa devotees should and must have their own *Guruswamy* guiding them all through the yatra to Sabarimala. Those who wish to know this science experientially, must not venture into this without the help of a *Guru*.

Who is Lord Ayyappa?

Lord Ayyappa is considered to be the incarnation of Lord Sastha. He is said to have taken birth, specifically for helping people in the *Kali Yuga* attain *mukthi*. Lord Sastha or Dharma Sastha is a very ancient deity, considered to be the son of Lord Shiva and Lord Vishnu (when he impersonated himself as Mohini). Therefore, Lord Ayyappa is said to be the combined form of Shiva, Vishnu and Shakti. The iconography of Sastha in different temples gives a clue as to the nature of the *chaitanyam* in that temple. Generally, in the ancient temples of Sastha where he appears with his consorts Purnakala and Pushkala, the temple will be open to all persons regardless of gender. The temples where he is in the form of a *Brahmachari*, has certain restrictions, especially for women in the menstrual age.

Of the six Sastha temples, one temple is located in Tirunelveli district of Tamil Nadu, and the rest are in Kerala. In Kerala, the five temples are known as the Pancha-Sastha temples. The origin of worship in the Tamil Nadu temple was initiated by sage Agasthya and the temples in Kerala, by sage Parashurama. So, they date back to thousands of years, to the time of the sages. While the historical details may or may not be a hundred percent correct, the *chaitanyam* in each of these spaces is undeniably vibrant even after so many years, and can be experienced by all those who are seeking to know it.

Every temple is a store-house of information. Volumes can be, and often has been written about the architecture, legend, mythology and history of temples. The legends, in particular, can be often misread if it is taken literally. Instead, if we attempt to understand the hidden clues in these metaphorical stories, we will discover a great many truths about the nature of the temple. Add to it, our own experience of the *chaitanyam* in the temple, can open up a whole other dimension of understanding. This is what I will attempt to uncover in the following pages.

One might wonder why we need to know about five other temples, when the issue is about Sabarimala. That's the whole point – if we want to fully understand Sabarimala, then it is a must to understand the associated Sastha temples, and how they are connected to Sabarimala.

Although many devotees consider Lord Ayyappa as a deity who fulfils their wishes, in reality, Lord Ayyappa and Sabarimala *Yatra* is all about the *nivritti marg* or the path of renunciation to attain *mukthi*. Understanding this is extremely essential for devotees, especially women in the reproductive age, who wish to become Ayyappa devotees and enter Sabarimala because this path requires them to renounce. Alternately, the process of renunciation will be triggered for them once they start this journey, whether or not they are prepared.

———∼∼∼———

CHAPTER 3

SORI MUTHAIYAN KOVIL – MULADHARA CHAKRA

————— ✕⧉✕ —————

Atop the scenic Pothigai hill in Tirunelveli district of Tamil Nadu, is an unassuming temple. It is situated along the banks of a beautiful river, Thamirabarani, which flows perennially. As you enter the temple, you will find peacocks casually strolling around. This is the Sori Muthaiyan Kovil, the first of the Sastha temples we visited. With hardly any devotees, we wondered if worship takes place here at all. Of course, we were there in June, and not during the festival seasons in Amavasya or the mandala period in December, when Ayyappa devotees start their pilgrimage from this place.

The Deity

The priest we met was happy to share whatever he knew about this temple. According to him, this is the *Mula* or *Adi Mula*, the starting point for Ayyappa devotees. It is here that the *Mala Dharanam* is undertaken; that is, a *mala* (chain to be worn around the neck) is given to the Ayyappa devotees by their *Guruswamy*. This marks the beginning of their 41-day *Vrata*[11] and pilgrimage to Sabarimala. This *mala* is not to be removed until the completion of the visit to Sabarimala and all related rituals.

In Sori Muthaiyan Kovil, Sastha is said to be in Adi Bhootanatha form, the controller of the *bhutas* (elements), indicating his role in *muladhara* which represents the earth element. On either side of Sastha are his two consorts, Purnakala and Pushkala. Adjoining the shrine of Sastha, to its left, is another shrine with a *Swayambhu Linga*, which is said to have been worshipped by sage Agastya.

The priest also informed us that the next set of temples to be visited before reaching Sabarimala are in the order of Achankovil, Aryankavu, Kulathupuzha and Erumeli, which is in the order of the *chakras - Swadisthana, Manipura, Anahata* and *Vishuddhi*. This

---

11 Ayyappa devotees are required to take up a 41-day Vrata before entering Sabarimala. During this time, strict rules are to be followed regarding lifestyle and diet. The devotees wear black, blue or orange garments, lead an ascetic's life, eat only sattvic vegetarian food, undertake prescribed rituals, observe strict celibacy and treat every person they meet as Ayyappa, the Lord Himself. Alcohol, smoking or any other such activity is prohibited and devotees are required to practice strict austerity, similar to the path of an ascetic (sage).

confirmed what Aravind *ji* had told us about the *Shat-Chakra*s being associated with the six temples of Sastha.

The Chaitanyam

The best way to get a taste of a space is to simply sit with eyes closed and observe the inner goings-on. This needs to be done with an open mind and without a pre-set agenda, which was easy because none of us knew what to expect in a temple that is associated with the *muladhara chakra*. When we set out to experience something, it always helps that we know very little theory so that it doesn't color our imagination.

Within about fifteen minutes of simply sitting still, I felt a distinct throbbing in the region below the abdomen. Initially I thought that it must be my imagination, so I let it pass, and continued to sit with my eyes closed. It happened a second time, and then a third time, and then again. This was no coincidence.

And I had thought that this place was too simple to have any impact! Lesson number one – never judge a temple by its building! The Sori Muthaiyan temple indeed works on the *muladhara chakra* located at the base of the spine. You can actually experience it if you can still the body and mind, just a little bit, and be present.

Image 1: Lord Sastha with Purnakala and Pushkala, at Sori Muthaiyan Kovil
(Image Courtesy: V. Aravind Subramanyam)

Significance for Devotees

During festivals, lakhs of villagers throng to this temple. This temple is popular among villagers as a go-to place to get rid of evil possessions and to seek protection. The surroundings of this temple have various deities, with the most prominent being that of Pattavarayan, who is worshipped as a protector of the cattle. Then there is Brahma Rakshasi, who is prayed to, for fertility. There is also the Illupai tree, which is said to swallow the offering of a bell by devotees who pray for a child. We were shown bells of all sizes that the tree trunk had grown over, or in other words 'swallowed'. The many deities, beliefs and associated legends, though fascinating, seem to distract from the shrine of Sastha and Swayambhu Linga. Looking back, it seems typical of what happens when a place is dominant in the *muladhara chakra*, where the play of *Maya* is very strong. People come here to overcome fear, insecurity, disease and to pray for fertility, health and wellbeing – all of which are functions of the *muladhara chakra* in the *pravritti marg* (action-oriented path).

The presence of Purnakala and Pushkala on either side of Sastha is also significant in understanding the nature of this place. Sometimes, they are referred to as *Jnana* (Knowledge) and *Bhakti* (Devotion). Often, devotees claim that they have *Bhakti* and hence, *Jnana* is not really essential and thereby dismiss the knowledge of *chakras* and *shastras*. Similarly, there are *Jnanis* who think that knowledge is sufficient and *Bhakti* is for the weaker mind. But the wise ones understand that real *Jnana* will nurture *Bhakti* and pure *Bhakti* will result in uncorrupt *Jnana*. In Sori Muthaiyan temple, we see that *Jnana* and *Bhakti* are separate from Sastha, indicating the gross (not-subtle) expressions of a person operating from *muladhara*. Whereas, as one goes higher up the *chakras*, we see that these two aspects are no longer separate entities and have become one with Sastha.

Those who consciously chose the *nivritti marg* (renunciation path) will begin to look beyond the outwardly possibilities and experience the pure *chaitanyam* in this place. That is why, for Ayyappa devotees who are supposed to be on the *nivritti marg*, this temple holds immense significance. It is the first place that will turn their attention inwards and help them rise beyond the insecurities of the material world, establishing them firmly on the path of *mukthi marg*.

It must be noted that my experience is probably just a tip of the iceberg, since I have not been initiated for this process. But unlike me, initiated Ayyappa devotees can surely experience this place much more powerfully. However, as we were told by the priest, only a small number of Ayyappa devotees come to this temple, and most don't even know the significance of this place.

Muladhara Chakra significance

The *Shat Chakra Nirupana* has a large number of verses, from verse 4 to 13, dedicated to describing the *muladhara chakra*. This is invariably the region which majority of us operate from. When our lives largely revolve around basic survival and procreation, a well energized *muladhara* becomes significant in successfully carrying out these processes.

The presiding male deity in *muladhara chakra* is Lord Brahma, the creator, and it is his creative aspects that come into play when *muladhara* is triggered. For those on the *pravritti marg*, the Shakti or feminine force called Devi Dakini, one of the *Bhairavis*, becomes more manifest. There is also *Svayambhu* in his Linga form, wrapped around which is key to Ultimate Realization, the *Kundalini*.

If one follows the rules set by a Guru and is on the *nivritti marg*, activation of the *muladhara chakra* becomes very significant. Only in the *muladhara*, can the *Kundalini shakti* be roused from its dormant state. *Kundalini Shakti* is considered as a sort of electric energy that remains coiled like a serpent in the *muladhara chakra*. When awakened, it runs along the spinal column, within the subtle *Sushumna nadi*[12], piercing through and activating each *chakra* in its path. According to Arthur Avalon's book "The Serpant Power', as *Kundalini* passes through each

---

12 Sushumna nadi is the most important and central nadi (subtle channel) for raising the Kundalini. Muladhara Chakra is located at the mouth of the Sushumna nadi. Once awakened, the Kundalini shoots up the spine via the Sushumna nadi.

chakra, it is said to create a sensation of intense heat, and when it leaves the *chakra*, the region it left feels cold. This is how we can experience the physiological effect of a spiritual process.

For an Ayyappa devotee, the first step in awakening the *Kundalini* will happen when they experience the *chaitanyam* in the Sori Muthaiyan Kovil, and undertake the *Mala Dharanam* from their Guru in this temple.

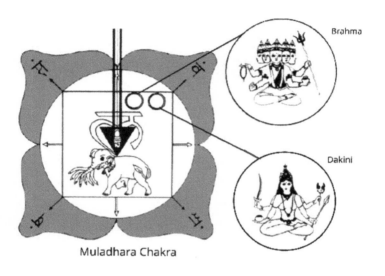

Muladhara Chakra

Figure 7: Muladhara Chakra
(Source: Swami Sivananda Radha, Kundalini Yoga for the West,
copyright 2005timelessbooks)

CHAPTER 4

ACHANKOVIL SREE DHARMASASTHA TEMPLE – SWADISTHANA CHAKRA

Deep in the forests of the Western Ghats in Kollam district of Kerala, in a small town, we find the Achankovil Sree Dharmasastha temple. From the moment we set foot in the temple premises, a smile will automatically form on our lips. There is something very pleasant, calming and soothing about the place. The priests too, are an embodiment of that pleasantness.

Given that my travel was by road for two days, I was quite disoriented and exhausted as I generally don't take well to travelling. But after visiting Achankovil, everything became smooth and easy. My health improved and I felt more alert than ever before. The tiredness of the journey seemed a thing of the past. This temple will have that effect on all who set foot here.

The Deity

In Achankovil, Sastha is the *Maha Vaidya*, the Great Healer, holding sandalwood paste in his right hand. He is represented as a King, full of *Aishwaryam* (abundant riches), granting the wishes of his subjects. Here too, Lord Sastha is seen with Purnakala and Pushkala on either side of him. As a *Grihastha* (married man), his *chaitanyam* in Achankovil is conducive for those who are on the worldly path of family and material life.

This is the only Sastha temple where they managed to still preserve the original idol brought by sage Parashurama. It is that same idol which is even now in worship here. Perhaps that is one of the reasons why it has such an unmistakable impact on anyone who walks in. Legend says that the main idol was brought from the Himalayas by Parashurama and is made with a special *Pancha Shila* (different from today's Panchaloha). When water or pure sandalwood touches this *vigraham*, it becomes medicinal in nature and can remove the poison in the body of the devotee. The water that is used for the *Abhiskeham*[13] becomes the healing *Theertha*[14].

---

13 Abhishekam is the term used to describe the sacred process of pouring water (or other liquids like Ghee, etc.) on the consecrated idol.

14 Theertham refers to the holy water which is given to devotees

Image 2: Lord Sastha with Purnakala and Pushkala, at Achankovil Temple

Image Courtesy: V. Aravind Subramanyam

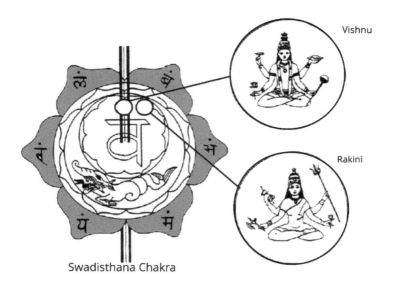

Figure 8: Swadisthana Chakra

(Source: Swami Sivananda Radha, Kundalini Yoga for the West, copyright 2005timelessbooks)

CHAPTER 5

ARYANKAVU SREE DHARMASASTHA TEMPLE – MANIPURA CHAKRA

⋯✕⇥⧉⇤✕⋯

Aryankavu Sree Dharmasastha temple gave me the most overwhelming experience, and I can still feel it even as I write this, two months after my visit. But it wasn't so easy or straightforward. Nothing in Aryankavu is. So, pardon my not-so-straightforward narration of this space, because that is how it happened here. The obstacles, the resolve, and finally, the overwhelming calmness is what one will experience here. Sometimes, all at once. And sometimes, once and for all.

The obstacles

Starting from Achankovil, by the time we reached the next temple in Aryankavu (about 40 kms away), it was already past noon and the shrine was closed until later in the evening. So, we hung around in the open area for a while and tried to peep in through the closed windows, just out of curiosity. We were discussing how it looked more like a marriage hall and were distracted by a peacock, prettily perched on top of the temple, flaunting its plume. And just like that, I started to experience cramps, similar to period pain, which is strange because I rarely experience period pain. Besides, my period was still a few days away. I assumed that it must have been something I ate, and we decided to return to the temple later in the evening.

But look at the strange turn of events. While wiling away time at a tourist spot nearby, Vyjayanthi had a minor fall, hurting her ankle and calf. So, we decided to postpone the visit and head back to the hotel where we stayed, about 100 kms away in Tirunelveli. Actually, we contemplated not coming back at all because Vyjayanthi was in pain all night and her leg had swollen. Besides, at the back of my mind, my earlier experience of the cramps, left me a little in doubt. An added reason for my hesitation was that this temple too has restrictions on the entry of women between the ages of 10 to 50 years, just like Sabarimala. But here, women are allowed to see the deity at a distance of about 10 meters from the shrine, in an area called the namaskara mantapa. So, while I couldn't anyway enter the shrine, we were considering whether or not Bhaskar and Vyjayanthi should take the trouble of coming back the next day for a visit. Unlike Achankovil, our first experience here did not make us feel very welcome.

Interestingly, Bhaskar kept intuitively suggesting that the nature of this place is such that it creates hurdles and puts us in a situation of doubt – to go or not to go! Once that awareness set in, we decided to break the jinx and go back the next day.

The resolve

In spite of spending the night being unsure, the next day, we decided to go and find out what this temple was all about. I made sure to remain on an empty stomach to avoid cramps. Vyjayanthi, despite being the oldest, was also the most adventurous among the three of us. Limping with a crape bandage and pain relief ointment, she too decided to join. This is in spite of the fact that the temple was some 35 feet below the ground, and there were steep steps to be taken down to reach the temple! But once we resolved to go back, new paths opened up, literally. What we had not noticed the previous day was a ramp from the other entrance which made it easier for Vyjayanthi. And this was only the first hurdle that was smoothly brushed aside; such a contrast from the previous day!

Overwhelming calmness

My plan was to declare my unsuitability to enter and remain in the namaskara mantapa area, while Vyjayanthi and Bhaskar went inside for the *darshan*. I thought of just waiting around until they returned.

But then the priest invited me to come closer to the entrance of the namaskara mantapa, so that I could get a better look. Apart from me, there were just about 3-4 other women. From where I stood, I could clearly see the deity and despite how resplendent He looked, something so compelling urged me to close my eyes and lift my hands up in the prayer position. I couldn't fathom why I felt so unusually overwhelmed. Automatically, the thought came to my mind – *Let me experience what You are.*

Few minutes later, the priest gently nudged me causing me to open my eyes and receive the *theertham*. Bhaskar and Vyjayanthi returned and we all exchanged a look. This deity had a strange pull, and we decided to sit down for a while and experience more of it. Within minutes of sitting in silence, I felt choked with tears unexpectedly, while smiling at the same time. The experience was too personal and not really possible to describe in words. It felt like sharing a moment of intense closeness with a loved one. As much as I would have loved to simply remain there, I instinctively knew that if I stayed there any longer, there was a chance I wouldn't want to return.

All at once, I understood what it means when we talk of *Bhakti* and the devotion of Meera for Lord Krishna, or that of Akkamahadevi for Lord Shiva. This is what women's bodies are capable of experiencing.

The pull is such that it becomes easy to leave everything else behind and simply remain in a state of devotion.

Over the next few days, it became all I could think of. And every time I thought about it, the experience came with it.

Bhaskar and I had the opportunity to meet Aravind *ji* in person, a few days later in Coimbatore. As I narrated my experience at Aryankavu, I again teared up. Thankfully, he was someone who could understand what this meant, and agreed that Aryankavu does have an unexplainable, overwhelming effect. Although men too feel the powerful draw of this place as Bhaskar and Aravind *ji* discussed, I felt that for women it was still, somehow, different; it was more personal.

After this visit, it became difficult to motivate myself to work or to attend to other things. Even writing this book, which I really enjoyed, became difficult. My mind kept thinking of ways in which I could go back and find some excuse to visit Aryankavu again. I even contemplated taking up some work at an office near the temple, so I could shift my base there. Such are the games the mind can play!

And then it occurred - if this could happen to me, with all my awareness, imagine what it could do to other women. Imagine how it would alter their family life, their responsibilities as a mother, as a wife.... Imagine.

The Legend

As we discussed with Aravind *ji* about what happened here, he recollected the legend of a young girl who was the daughter of a merchant from Saurastra, and accompanied her father during his business visit to this region. She instantly fell in love with the deity in this temple and asked her father if she could remain there while he finished his work and returned. After completing the business, as the merchant was returning, he was chased by a wild elephant in the forest. Suddenly a hunter appeared on the scene and drove away the elephant. Pleased, the merchant presented the hunter a silk shawl. But the hunter in return asked if the merchant would marry his daughter to the hunter. The merchant immediately gave his consent, and the hunter said that they should meet at Aryankavu temple the next day.

However, the daughter's love for Sastha was such that, by the time her father returned, he only found her idol next to that of Sastha. She had merged into Him. The merchant found that the silk shawl which he presented to the hunter the previous day, was now worn by the idol of Sastha. This revealed that the hunter was none other than Lord Sastha and that He had accepted the merchant's daughter. So even though the photograph in the temple shows her to the left of Sastha, the *vigraham* does not show her presence. Inside the shrine, Sastha is simply sitting like a *Brahmachari,* with a smile that seems to know what will happen to those who come in contact with him.

Even today, there is a festival to celebrate the *Kalyanam* (marriage) of the deity with this young girl and that's why the temple is designed like a marriage hall. A group arrives from Saurastra as the bride's party, and is received by the temple authorities who represent the groom's party. But the festivities always conclude with the groom's decision to not marry, and take to the path of renunciation and *Brahmacharya*. Aravind *ji* is of the opinion that *Kalyanam* here does not mean a physical marriage, but the merging of the devotee with the deity.

This story reminded us of the confusion that we encountered when we wanted to visit Aryankavu. Perhaps for Ayyappa devotees also, coming here is not so easy. They need to make up their mind and remain firm in that decision. As Bhaskar summarized, this place has a significant pull for men, and once they come in contact with the deity, it puts them in the path of renunciation. *Vairagya* (detachment) becomes easy once we come to this place and the pull of materialistic life is weakened. This is how Aryankavu assists the Ayyappa devotees in the path of *Brahmacharya* and prepares them for Sabarimala.

Image 3: Lord Sastha at Aryankavu temple
(Image Courtesy: V. Aravind Subramanyam)

The impact on women

For women, the essence of merging with the deity is what permeates the *chaitanyam* in this place. My intention in describing this in such detail is because women need to know the type of impact it can have on their emotional and physical health. Emotionally, women will develop a sense of detachment to family and worldly affairs. This is very likely the reason why even menopausal women who decide to become Ayyappa devotees and go to Sabarimala, can only be initiated by their husbands. Not even a Guru is allowed to initiate them. This tradition is there to ensure that the husband understands that his wife will no longer be devoted to him or the family, but rather to Lord Ayyappa, and grants her wish to go on that path.

Physically, such spaces create a conflict with the menstrual and reproductive process. Although my period came a week after my visit, as scheduled, I experienced the same type of cramping sensation that I had, when I first visited Aryankavu. I had to force myself to not think of the place, so that my body would stop reacting to that experience. It was as though my body was resisting menstruation.

Manipura Chakra significance

For those on the *pravritti marg*, *manipura chakra* invokes the Devi Lakini who resides in this *chakra*. She is considered to be the benefactress of all. By meditating upon her in this *chakra*, material success, power and ambition is manifested. But for those on the *nivritti marg*, it is the first step to a cross-over of sorts to the 'other side'.

The presiding male deity in *manipura chakra* is Rudra. Though Rudra is generally attributed with fierce qualities, in *Shat-Chakra-Nirupana*, he is described as seeming to be white with ashes smeared upon him, like an ancient ascetic (sage). He is said to be the destroyer of creation. The presence of Rudra here, like a sage, is an indication of this *chakra* putting people on the path of renunciation, if they chose the *nivritti marg*. *Manipura chakra* is where that transformation begins to happen.

For me, the experience in Aryankavu helped me gain an important insight into why women in the menstruating age are discouraged from undertaking this pilgrimage to Sabarimala. The process of menstruation is intrinsic to creation. But the path of spirituality necessitates the ability to break the cycle of birth and re-birth to achieve *mukthi*. Hence, for women in the menstruating age, the spiritual path involving renunciation and detachment, comes in the way of their reproductive abilities.

Unlike women's menstrual cycles which are involuntary, for men, controlling the process of creation is voluntary. Therefore, for men in this path, observing celibacy for a period of 41-days prior to visiting Sabarimala, will serve the purpose, without putting their bodies in conflict with the spiritual process.

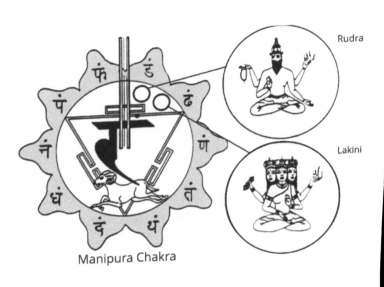

Rudra

Lakini

Manipura Chakra

Figure 9: Manipura Chakra

(Source: Swami Sivananda Radha, Kundalini Yoga for the West, copyright 2005timelessbooks)

CHAPTER 6

SHREE KULATHUPUZHA BALA SASTHA TEMPLE – ANAHATA CHAKRA

Situated around 25 kms from Aryankavu, is the Bala Sastha Temple at Kulathupuzha. The temple is located in the Kulathupuzha reserve forest range, in the east of Kollam district. We had decided to visit this temple on the same day as Aryankavu, and we reached Kulathupuzha just in time for the evening *aarathi*. If a temple could ever be described as cozy and grand at the same time, then this was it. The entire temple is designed for a child – Bala Sastha (young Sastha). The roof is low keeping in mind the height of a child, and the place is decorated in such a way that it would be attractive for children. Warmth, light and compassion, all of these burst forth in this place.

The deity

In Kulathupuzha, Lord Sastha is worshipped as an infant, with his parents close to him. Krishna (an avatar of Vishnu) is present just outside as the mother of Balasastha. In the sanctum, on the left, Shiva is also present, as the father of Balasastha.

The place therefore has the energy of parents' love for their child. During our visit, though there were only two other devotees, both had brought along their children for the visit. In this temple, it is believed, that children are taken care of. Whether it is an ailment, the tension of exams or any other problem faced by children, parents bring them here to seek help. Childless couples also come here to pray for begetting a child.

The Chaitanyam

Within moments of closing my eyes while the *aarathi* began, I distinctly sensed a throbbing sensation in the heart region. The throbbing was there throughout, whether my eyes were open or closed. And it remained for a while even after we left the place. This was the strongest sensation I had felt with respect to any of the *chakras* so far. Afterall, this temple triggered the *anahata chakra*, situated in the region of the heart.

Significance of Anahata Chakra

Anahata Chakra has Isvara (Isa/Shiva) as the presiding male deity who is described as an abode of mercy. He can create, maintain and destroy the world. Devi Kakini is the female deity, meditating upon whom, dispels fear.

Image 4: Bala Shastha at Kulathupuzha temple
(Image Courtesy: V. Aravind Subramanyam)

This *chakra* is described as the *kalpavruksha*, the wishing tree, meaning everything that one longs for is obtained, and more. *Shat-Chakra-Nirupana* says that a person who meditates on Isvara here becomes the foremost of Yogis, wisest among the wise, full of noble deeds, and dearest to women. At the same time, he has complete control over his senses and his thoughts are intensely concentrated on Brahman.

On the *nivritti marg*, emotions of compassion, love and feeling of oneness permeates this *chakra*. The presence of Sastha here as a child is representative of these emotions which is more likely to be felt towards an infant. When *anahata* is open, one can experience it by the way it becomes easier to understand others' perspective and how it becomes effortless to feel compassionate towards all things – man, animal and nature. This is an important step for a spiritual aspirant – to be able to love effortlessly, and see oneself in all aspects of creation.

Figure 10: Anahata Chakra
(Source: Swami Sivananda Radha, Kundalini Yoga for the West,
copyright 2005timelessbooks)

CHAPTER 7

ERUMELI SHRI DHARMA SASTHA TEMPLE – VISHUDDHI CHAKRA

The fifth of the *Shat-Chakra* temples associated with Sabarimala is in the town of Erumeli in Kottayam district of Kerala. We were able to visit the temples here in September 2019. There are two temples here - Petta Sri Dharmasastha temple, known as *Kochambalam* (small temple) and Erumeli Sree Dharmasastha Temple, known as *Valiyambalam* (big temple). Even though many Ayyappa devotees are not aware of the earlier four temples, they all know about Erumeli as it is an important destination before starting the trek to Sabarimala. This destination is of particular importance to the first-timers, who are called *Kanni-Swami*. Erumeli is known for the *Petta Thullal*, a sort of tribal dance which *Kanni-swamis* have to mandatorily perform. There is also a mosque opposite to the *Kochambalam* which is circumambulated by the devotees. This is done as a sign of respect to Vavar, who some say, was a trusted lieutenant of Ayyappa. During our visit, we noticed a muslim auto driver pray at the *Valiyambalam* and receive the *prasadam* as if it was part of his daily activities.

The deity

The *Kochambalam* has Sastha as a warrior ready to strike down enemies. The *Valiyambalam* Sastha seems to be dressed up for the *Petta Thullal*, which is the significant aspect of these temples. The *Petta Thullal* takes place in the *mandalam* period during the months of November to January. This event is related to the *purana* story of the slaying of the demoness Mahishi by Sastha. The *Petta Thullal* is thus a reminder and a replay of the ecstatic dance of the local people after the demoness was killed. Symbolically, it is perhaps the representation of the slaying of inner vices that happen as part of the Sabarimala yatra. There is also the possibility that one in whom the *vishuddhi chakra* is active, will tend to attract spirits. Therefore, the loud noise and dance during the *Petta Thullal* is metaphorically meant to drive away the spirits. The slaying of demoness Mahishi is possibly symbolic of this.

The Chaitanyam

The temples at Erumeli are simple in form and experience. Unlike the overwhelming Aryankavu or the unmistakable bliss at Achankovil and Kulathupuzha,

Image 5: Lord Shastha at Erumeli Temple
(Image Courtesy: V. Aravind Subramanyam)

here, the experience was a lot milder. However, I felt a weak sensation in the region of the throat that could have easily gone unnoticed, had I not been so aware of what to expect here. Perhaps, to really experience the significance of Erumeli, one must visit during the *Petta Thullal*. However, we did experience something significant just a few kilometers from Erumeli.

Of all the routes to Sabarimala, the route via Erumeli is considered to be the most difficult, especially if one chose to trek via the forest for a distance of about 60 kms. Yet, it is preferred by many devotees since this is the route that Ayyappa is said to have taken when he went to slay Mahishi. About 4 kms from Erumeli is *Perur Thodu*, a place where Ayyappa is believed to have rested during his expedition. This place is also important as it marks the start of the climb to Sabarimala. The forest beyond *Perur Thodu* is known as *Poongavanam*, meaning garden. There is a small shrine here, and even though we only passed this place en route to our next destination, we could distinctly sense a different sort of vibration here. From here, we were told that the trek to the eighteen hills begin, taking devotees to Sabarimala. I have heard stories of devotees who at first doubted their own ability to trek this far in the forest, but at the end of it, they always made a promise to return and trek again next year. The forest and the shrine are not like any other experience. There is something here that will change a person and the way we experience divinity. It can only be understood by one who experiences it.

Significance of Vishuddhi Chakra

The Erumeli Sree Dharma Sastha temples are associated with the *vishuddhi chakra*. The *Shat-Chakra Nirupana* says that there are 72,000 *nadis* emerging from the *kanda*, a bulbous region in the uro-genital (*muladhara*). Of all the *nadis*, the three important ones are *Ida*, *Pingala* and *Sushumna*. The *Sushumna nadi* clings to the stalk of *Sakhini nadi* that starts at the *kanda* and goes till the throat (*vishuddhi*), from where *Sakhini* branches and one goes to left ear and the other to the crown.

The female deity at *vishuddhi chakra* is called Devi Sakhini, who is the gatekeeper to the great door of *mukthi* for a devotee who has gained control over his senses. Her form is of light (*Jyoti-swarupa*). The presiding male deity in this *chakra* is *Sadashiva* as *Ardhanarishwara*, with one half of his body being white (representing Shiva), and the other being golden (representing Gauri).

For one attempting to raise the *Kundalini*, it is said that external processes can take one as far as the *vishuddhi*. Further ascent from the *vishuddhi* is said to be difficult, and requires, among other things, the grace of the *Guru*. For Ayyappa devotees, the extent to which they have been able to gain mastery or control over their mind and senses at this level, will determine how much closer they are to merging with Ayyappa at Sabarimala.

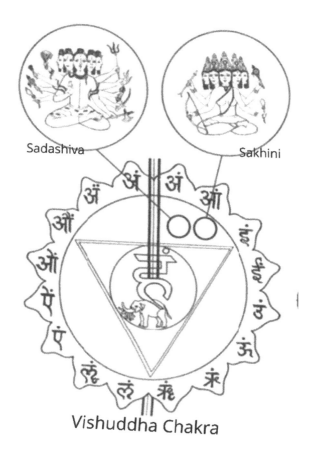

Sadashiva

Sakhini

Vishuddha Chakra

Figure 11: Vishuddha Chakra
(Source: Veeraswamy Krishnaraj, Commentary on Shat Chakra Nirupana)

CHAPTER 8

SREE DHARMA SASTHA TEMPLE, SABARIMALA – AJNA CHAKRA

---×-⟨≫≪⟩-×---

All through the journey to Erumeli, I kept wondering what it would be like to be able to visit Sabarimala and have the *darshan* of Lord Ayyappa. My visit to Erumeli was part of the work we had taken up to support flood affected families in the vicinity of Sabarimala. We were hosted by Hariharaputra Seva Trust, who helped us in this initiative. Just before we left, our hosts gave us something very special. Directly from the Sabarimala kovil, we received the Ayyappa *prasadam*, a small crown that was placed on the *murthi* of Lord Ayyappa, a few sacred threads and other items used during worship. It was as though Lord Ayyappa himself had acknowledged our work and sent His blessings. What more could I ask for?

Sabarimala - the *mala* (hill) of Sabari. Sabari was a women ascetic from ancient times who was found meditating on the hill. When Lord Ayyappa decided to attain *samadhi*, he chose this spot and merged into the idol of Sastha.

For a place that is named after a woman ascetic, the notion of how women devotees could cause disturbance to Lord Ayyappa residing here, is but, a natural question. When the case was on in the supreme court of India to remove the restriction on women of menstruating age from entering Sabarimala, the chief argument by those defending the restriction was that women will disturb Lord Ayyappa who is a *Naishtika Brahmachari*, meaning, one who has taken the vow of *Brahmacharya* for life. The assumption that such a Great One would be prone to disturbance by common women folk, shows the little that has been understood about what it means when a deity is considered to be a *Brahmachari*. Those who spoke about Lord Ayyappa attributed to him their own lack of control and colored him like them. Such arguments are not just insulting to women, but also to Lord Ayyappa.

Brahmacharya

A seasoned *Brahmachari* is one who has supreme control over all his senses. It is not just about celibacy as is known in western world. It is about absolute supremacy over his emotions and a certain solidity of personality. Even to say that he practices 'restraint' would be incorrect, because restraint means that there is effort involved in holding back. For an accomplished

Brahmachari, it is but natural to be unshakable. One who has attained to that state, cannot be troubled by anything at all. Lord Ayyappa represents this aspect in its fullest form as a *Naishtika Brahmachari*. In the presence of such a One, it is not He who will be disturbed, rather it is those who come to Him unaware and unprepared.

The *chaitanyam* in Sabarimala is such that the aspect of *Brahmacharya* permeates the place, and that is why Ayyappa devotees have to raise themselves through strict austerities to be able to remain in his presence. Therefore, it is not just women in the menstrual age group who are restricted from entering Sabarimala, but also any male (or female) devotee who has not undergone the 41-day *Vrata* and *Brahmacharya* practice, are also restricted from climbing the holy 18 steps (*padinettam padi*) and having the *darshan* of Ayyappa.

Physiology of Spirituality

The physical process that the human body experiences while pursuing spirituality is the transformation of the *shukra*, the human seed contained in the sexual fluids of semen (in men) and menstrual blood (in women), into the subtle *Ojas*. Sushrutha Samhita[15] text describes *Ojas* as being present in the reproductive energy that lies latent as the essence of the food we consume. It is

---

15 Sushrutha Samhita is a treatise on Ayurveda

Image 6: Lord Ayyappa, at Sabarimala

(Source: www.stateofkerala.in)

the presence of *Ojas* that results in vitality, cellular immunity and a healthy glow. This glow is what is sometimes perceived as the 'aura' of a person, especially one who is a seasoned *Brahmachari*.

An important aspect of *Brahmacharya* is to be able to withhold the human seed and transform it into subtler forms, by raising it higher up the *chakras*. Therefore, celibacy and prevention of emitting the seed (sperm) becomes important for male devotees to fully experience the spiritual process. However, for women in the menstrual age, the seed, which is the egg, is involuntarily released during menstruation.

The female counterpart to male semen retention is the cessation of menstruation, which is taught in rare Tantra and Taoist practices. In such practices, women are taught to re-channelize their sexual energies and preserve their vital energy, *prana*, which is lost every month during menstruation. A book[16] by Mantak Chai, claims to teach women this technique, through which menstruation is greatly reduced or ceases to occur.

Please note that I do not support or recommend any unnatural suppression of menstruation as it could cause several untoward problems. The masters who know this technique are very few and unless one is sure of the Guru's ability and are prepared for the

---

16 Chai, Mantak: Healing Love through the Tao: Cultivating Female Sexual Energy, 2005

consequences, one must not attempt it. This aspect has been mentioned here only to give readers an idea that such a technique exists and it is possible for certain practices to alter women's menstrual ability.

Playing with sexual energy is akin to playing with fire. One must be in absolute control of the senses and in a state of complete awareness. Otherwise, too many things can go wrong, as we see in people following yoga and 'chakra activation' without proper guidance, and not knowing what to do with the surge of sexual energy that happens when kundalini is roused. That is why, traditionally, such processes are only done as per a Guru's guidance and are always associated with deep faith and devotion. Only by offering all one's emotions to a deity and complete submission, can one overcome the intense sexual pull that such processes can cause. And so, processes like Sabarimala demand complete devotion to Lord Ayyappa, and separation from the opposite gender.

Sabarimala temple has been conceived with the intention of making it possible for devotees to experience spiritual enlightenment, through all the rules, austerities and restrictions imposed during the 41-days of the Vrata. The practice of being able to contain sexual energy and withhold the human seed is at the core of this experience. Therefore, if women in the menstruating age take the Ayyappa Vrata and enter Sabarimala, they will experience the withholding of the seed as a struggle to menstruate, resulting in menstrual and reproductive disorders.

Ajna Chakra Significance

Sabarimala is associated with the *ajna chakra*, which is the command center of the mind. It is here that the command of the Guru *(ajna)* is received from above. Gaining control over this *chakra* means one becomes like a *Brahmachari*. Alternately, one practicing *Brahmacharya* will have an active *ajna chakra*. The *ajna chakra* is associated with great intellect, intelligence and natural leadership skills. All spiritual leaders whose mere presence will draw crowds are classic examples of those with active *ajna chakras*.

The presiding female deity here is Devi Hakini, who is six faced, considered as pure minded *(Suddha-Citta)*, grants boons and dispels fear. Paramashiva (Shambhu) in *hamsa-rupa* is present here. There is also the *Itara Linga* here, inside which is Shiva united with Shakti. This is the place where the three nadis, Ida, Pingala and Sushumna, merge and flow upwards.

In the *nivritti marg*, this is the region where the spiritual aspirant ceases to be an aspirant and realizes his/her oneness with the cosmos. If Ayyappa devotees follow all the rules and experience the rising of *Kundalini* through the *Shat-Chakra* temples, then Sabarimala is the place where they will experience the Ultimate Union with the Divine. Just as Ayyappa

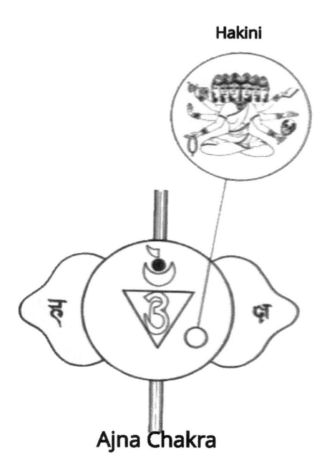

Figure 12: Ajna Chakra

(Source: Veeraswamy Krishnaraj, Commentary on Shat Chakra Nirupana)

merged into the idol of Sastha at Sabarimala, Ayyappa devotees too have a chance at experiencing such a oneness with the Divine.

Physiologically speaking, raising the *kundalini* upwards and activation of the *ajna chakra* can have very different impact on women and men. When *ajna chakra* is triggered, it acts on the pituitary gland. The pituitary gland plays an important role in reproductive process for both men and women, by secreting two hormones called Luteinizing Hormone (LH) and Follicle-Stimulating Hormone (FSH). In men, LH stimulates testosterone production from the interstitial cells of the testes. So, an activated *ajna chakra* in men corresponds to a well-functioning pituitary gland and production of testosterone.

Similarly, in women too, LH stimulates testosterone production. Unlike men, however, women must have much lower concentrations of testosterone and it only rises at the time around ovulation. In women, testosterone is important for bone strength and to increase sexual libido, necessary for procreation. The female hormone estrogen is made from testosterone and other adrenal hormones. Without the ability of women's bodies to make testosterone, they cannot make estrogen. Estrogen is what causes ovulation, followed by menstruation.

Spaces such as Sabarimala work primarily on the *ajna chakra*. For women, if the *ajna chakra* alone is energized and if *swadisthana* and *muladhara* are not sufficiently active, the ovaries will eventually become dysfunctional and unable to convert the testosterone into female hormones. This could result in lesser or inadequate production of estrogen by the ovaries and hence, excess testosterone.

While an increase in testosterone is not harmful for men, even a slight increase in testosterone in a woman's body can suppress normal menstruation and ovulation. The release of hormones from the pituitary gland is influenced by a feedback loop from the ovaries during the menstrual cycle. However, in the case of dysfunctional ovaries, such a feedback does not happen, resulting in the pituitary producing excess LH and consequently, excess testosterone. Some of the symptoms of excess testosterone in females include excessive facial hair (Hirsutism), deepened masculine voice and difficulty reproducing owing to disorders such as Polycyctic Ovarian Symptom (PCOS) and Polycyctic Ovarian Disorder (PCOD).

Further, a dominant *ajna chakra* will alter the internal *doshas* and the functions they govern. This is one of the reasons why those on the spiritual path have strict diet restrictions, so that processes such as digestion and excretion, governed by specific *doshas (Samana Vayu* and *Apana Vayu)*, will not be severely affected. For women with a dominant *ajna chakra*, the downward flowing *apana vayu*, which causes menstrual blood to flow down and out, will be altered, causing difficulty in menstruation. Over a period of time, such alteration of the subtle bodily forces could result in a reversal in the direction of *apana vayu* causing retrograde menstruation in disorders such as endometriosis.

These are the answers for those who have asked the question "Why are women in the menstrual age restricted from entering Sabarimala?"

CHAPTER 9

THE SPIRITUAL PATH FOR WOMEN

Women might ask that if the path of renunciation and journey to Sabarimala is not open for them owing to their reproductive ability, then what is the alternative? What is the spiritual path for women in the menstruating age? Is waiting for menopause the only answer?

The beauty of the Hindu tradition is that there is always something unique for each of us, which takes into account our physical and emotional abilities. While devotion to Lord Ayyappa is the path of strict austerities and renunciation of desires, there is another path where the opposite happens, which is, fulfilment of desires. This is the path of *Devi Upasana*, devotion to the Great Mother. As a Mother, she does not deny our desires nor does she ask us to wait and renounce. Her method is to fulfil our desires, thereby completing our *karma*, and thus leading us to liberation. Though the end objective is the same in both paths, the journey is vastly different.

I understood this when I visited the well-known Kamakhya temple in Assam, which is a powerful *shakti peeth*. The timing of my visit couldn't have been better. A week after I returned from visiting the first four temples of Sastha, I was feeling strangely disinterested in pursuing matters of work and worldly affairs – a result of experiencing Aryankavu, no doubt! But visiting the Kamakhya temple changed the complete course of my activities.

She again called me when I decided to visit the Sastha temples at Erumeli. During that trip, I ended up visiting three very powerful Bhadrakali temples, although it was unplanned. In fact, something strange happened that is perhaps connected to why I could not experience the Erumeli Sastha temples in a deeper way. The night before I visited Erumeli, I was taken to witness a *Guruthi* at the Valliyamkavu temple in Kottayam district. The *Guruthi* which I witnessed was a ritual involving sacrifice and invocation of Kali. Although the tradition had shifted from sacrifice of animals to symbolic breaking of pumpkins and using vermillion powder for blood, the process was still mesmerizing. While standing there, I closed my eyes for a few minutes, and I just swayed forward. It kept happening again and again. I noticed the same thing happening for Bhaskar who had accompanied me. Her presence was felt among the hundred odd people who had gathered there in pin-drop silence that night.

I later learnt that during the Sabarimala season, although this temple remains open, the *Guruthi* does not take place. *Guruthi's* are mostly performed for fulfilment of desires and success in material pursuits. Goddess Kali is invoked to fulfil the desires of devotees. This is very much the opposite of the path of renunciation that Ayyappa devotees are required to take. And that is probably why the *Guruthi* is not performed during the Ayyappa season. It is likely that the impact of the *Guruthi* that I witnessed just a night before visiting Erumeli Sastha temples, was such that it overpowered the experience at Erumeli.

Temples and Gender

Spirituality, in its ultimate form, knows no gender. But for most of us, reaching that stage is not easy. Until we transcend our gender identities and reach the stage where we identify ourselves as neither male nor female, gender matters very much. The masculine and feminine energies consecrated in temples could have a different impact on each of us, based on our gender identity.

It has been my experience and observation that some temples with feminine deities have a comforting effect on those who identify themselves as female. Whereas the same feminine temple can have an overwhelming attractive quality for those who identify themselves as male. It is not uncommon that many *Devi Upasaks* are therefore, men.

Similarly, some temples of powerful male deities have an overwhelming effect on women for whom *Bhakti* takes over every other aspect of life. They simply fall in love with the deity. For men, such temples help them introspect and make the journey inward to the Source.

According to the way in which these spaces impact men and women, customs and traditions have been arrived at. Recognizing this difference and appreciating the possibilities available to both men and women are crucial if one is serious about spirituality.

If the final goal is *mukthi*, then should we not take the path that will get us there with least difficulty, instead of fighting to forcibly enter another's path, and facing physical and emotional difficulties in the process?

———~~~———

Bibliography

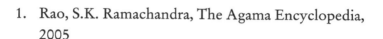

1. Rao, S.K. Ramachandra, The Agama Encyclopedia, 2005

2. Kramrisch, Stella. The Hindu Temple, Vol 1, 1946

3. Purnananda, Swami. Shat Chakra Nirupana, 1526 CE

4. Avalon, Arthur (Woodroof, John). The Serpant Power: The Secrets of Tantric and Shaktic Yoga, 1974

5. Leadbeater, C.W. The Chakras, 1927

6. Subramanyam, Aravind. Shri Maha Sastha Vijayam

7. Subramanyam, Aravind. Shri Boothanatha Geetha

8. Chai, Mantak: Healing Love through the Tao: Cultivating Female Sexual Energy, 2005

9. Sushruta. Sushruta Samhita